# JAMES *Buchanan*

# JAMES *Buchanan*

## OUR FIFTEENTH PRESIDENT

*By Gerry and Janet Souter*

SPIRIT
of America™

*The Child's World®, Inc.*
*Chanhassen, Minnesota*

# JAMES *Buchanan*

*Published in the United States of America by The Child's World®, Inc.*
PO Box 326 • Chanhassen, MN 55317-0326 • 800-599-READ • www.childsworld.com

*Acknowledgments*
   The Creative Spark: Mary Francis-DeMarois, Project Director; Elizabeth Sirimarco Budd, Series Editor;
   Robert Court, Design and Art Direction; Janine Graham, Page Layout; Jennifer Moyers, Production

   The Child's World®, Inc.: Mary Berendes, Publishing Director; Red Line Editorial, Fact Research;
   Cindy Klingel, Curriculum Advisor; Robert Noyed, Historical Advisor

*Photos*
   Cover: White House Collection, courtesy White House Historical Association; Bettmann/Corbis: 16,
   27, 30; ©Corbis: 29, 32; Courtesy of Dickinson College, Carlisle, Pennsylvania: 8; Courtesy of the
   Hermitage, Nashville, Tennessee: 14; The Huntington Library, San Marino, California: 29; Courtesy of
   the James Buchanan Foundation, Lancaster, Pennsylvania: 6, 10, 28; Courtesy of the Lancaster County
   Historical Society, Lancaster, Pennsylvania: 11 (both images), 22, 36; Collections of the Library of
   Congress: 13, 19, 20-21, 23, 24, 26; Courtesy of Mercersburg Academy: 7; North Wind Picture
   Archives; Stock Montage: 35

*Registration*
   The Child's World®, Inc., Spirit of America™, and their associated logos are the sole property and
   registered trademarks of The Child's World®, Inc.

*Library of Congress Cataloging-in-Publication Data*
   Souter, Gerry.
      James Buchanan : our fifteenth president / by Gerry and Janet Souter.
         p. cm.
      Includes bibliographical references and index.
      ISBN 1-56766-852-6 (alk. paper)
      1. Buchanan, James, 1791–1868—Juvenile literature.  2. Presidents—United States—Biography—
   Juvenile literature. [1. Buchanan, James, 1791-1868. 2. Presidents.]  I. Souter, Janet, 1940-    .
   II. Title.
      E437 .S68 2000
      973.6'8'092—dc21
                                                            00-011454

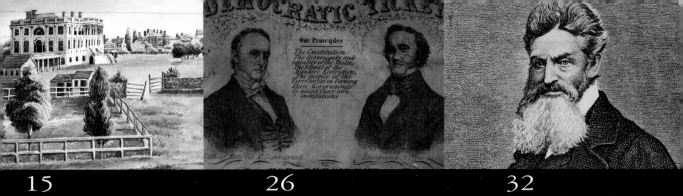

# Contents

| *Chapter* ONE | From Schoolboy to Politician | 6 |
| *Chapter* TWO | The Road to the Senate | 10 |
| *Chapter* THREE | Approaching Storm | 22 |
| *Chapter* FOUR | A Wearisome Presidency | 28 |
| | Time Line | 38 |
| | Glossary Terms | 40 |
| | Our Presidents | 42 |
| | Presidential Facts | 46 |
| | For Further Information | 47 |
| | Index | 48 |

# From Schoolboy to Politician

*James Buchanan entered the presidency during one of the most difficult periods in history. The northern and southern states were fighting bitterly about the right to own slaves, and the nation teetered on the edge of war.*

JAMES BUCHANAN, THE 15TH U.S. PRESIDENT, was the firstborn son of Elizabeth Speer Buchanan and James Buchanan. He was born on April 23, 1791, in Cove Gap, Pennsylvania. Five years later, the Buchanan family moved to the town of Mercersburg. Young James's father was a successful shopkeeper. He also kept a small farm. In Mercersburg, Mr. Buchanan purchased a two-story building that served as both the family's home and his store. From his father, young James learned about running a business and about the importance of keeping accurate records. His mother taught him to enjoy poetry. Together she and James read the works of popular poets of the time.

At age 16, James was already prepared for college. He enrolled at Dickinson College in

the nearby town of Carlisle. Because his parents had provided him with an excellent education, he entered college as a junior, a third-year student. Although he studied and received good grades, James often found himself in trouble with his teachers. They thought he spent too much time having fun with his friends. Near the end of his time at Dickinson, his teachers threatened to make him leave school because of his behavior. Dr. John King, a pastor and a Buchanan

*The cabin where Buchanan was born was simple and rustic. As his father grew more successful, the family moved to a larger home in the town of Mercersburg, Pennsylvania.*

*James Buchanan was intelligent enough to enter Dickinson College (above) at age 16, but he may not have been mature enough. In an effort to "fit in," James joined his friends in playing pranks on their teachers. Even though he earned high grades, he was often in trouble.*

family friend, spoke to the school. Fortunately, the school agreed to let James finish his final year. During that time, he stayed out of trouble and earned high grades.

After leaving Dickinson, James decided to study law. He was the oldest son of the family's eight children. His father wanted James to have a good income in case he ever needed to help support the family. This interest would stay with James the rest of his life. He was so eager to succeed that he worked and studied hard all day. Then in the evenings, he practiced making speeches after he finished work.

He understood that a lawyer must be comfortable speaking in front of people. James passed his law exams in 1812, and he was ready to open his own law office. Within a short time, he had a busy and successful career in Lancaster, Pennsylvania.

At about the time that James opened his law office, the United States and Great Britain were at war. In 1814, James decided to run for the state legislature. A legislature is the part of a government that makes laws. But in August, he heard that the British had attacked Washington, D.C.—the nation's capital. They had set the president's home, the Capitol, and other government buildings on fire. Then they marched on toward the city of Baltimore. James decided to volunteer for the army. Fortunately, the United States soon began to win important battles. He only served as a soldier for a few weeks before the British were no longer a threat. By late December, the two nations had signed a peace treaty, an agreement to end the war. Shortly before that, James had been elected to the Pennsylvania House of Representatives. He was about to start a new career in politics, the work of the government.

# Chapter TWO

# The Road to the Senate

*Buchanan was a young man of 24 years when he entered the Pennsylvania House of Representatives.*

WHEN BUCHANAN JOINED THE LEGISLATURE, a representative's **term** lasted only one year. So in the autumn of 1815, he ran for a second term and won. During his time in the legislature, Buchanan argued that there should not be a single, large bank that controlled all of the government's money. He believed it was wrong to let a few people have so much power. The matter would not be settled for more than a decade, when Andrew Jackson was the president.

In 1816, Buchanan decided to leave politics and return to his law practice in Lancaster. Two years after he left the legislature, he met Ann Coleman, a young woman from a wealthy Lancaster family. He asked her to marry him in 1819, and Ann accepted. But she and her family canceled the wedding plans in November of that year. She had heard terrible rumors that James didn't love her, and that he was only marrying her for the family's money. Then, while on a visit to Philadelphia, Ann became ill and died.

Buchanan was heartbroken. He sent letters to her father, asking to see Ann's body before she was buried. "I feel that happiness has fled from me forever," he wrote. Mr. Coleman returned the letters unopened.

*In 1818, Buchanan met Ann Coleman. The couple fell in love and planned to marry. Unfortunately, Ann called off the engagement. Buchanan would remain a bachelor for the rest of his life.*

*Buchanan's law office was located on East King Street in Lancaster, Pennsylvania.*

▶ James Buchanan is the only president who never married. He is known as "The Bachelor President."

▶ In the 1820s, some Americans formed the American Colonization Society. Its goal was to send all blacks in the United States to Liberia, a newly formed country in Africa where they could live in freedom.

Buchanan was so sad that he left Lancaster and his law practice. He was gone for several weeks, not wanting to stay in a town filled with unhappy memories. Finally, a friend suggested that he run for the U.S. Congress. Perhaps that would help to take his mind off Ann's death. In 1820, Buchanan was elected to the U.S. House of Representatives. He moved to Washington, D.C., to start an exciting new life.

Buchanan served in the House of Representatives for 10 years. During that time, trouble began to brew between the northern and southern states. Many Northerners hated slavery. Southerners, however, had no intention of giving up the free labor their slaves provided. The year before Buchanan was elected, Missouri settlers asked the government to make their **territory** a state. The problem was that no one could decide whether it should be a slave state or a free state. Northerners did not want slavery to spread. Southerners did not want the nation to have more free states than slave states. Congress could not solve the problem that year.

In 1820, the people of Maine wanted to form a state as well. Finally, Congress made a **compromise.** It decided that Maine would be admitted to the **Union** as a free state. Missouri would be a slave state. This way, the number of free and slave states would remain equal. There would be 12 of each. In addition, Congress divided the continent in half at a **latitude** of 36 degrees, 30 minutes. From that time forward, slavery would be legal in all areas south of that latitude. In all areas north of it, slavery would be illegal. The boundary came to symbolize not only the border between the North and the South, but also between slavery and freedom. This decision became known as the Missouri Compromise.

*Southerners believed they could not run their large farms, called plantations, without slaves. They were furious that some people from the North wanted to interfere with the Southern way of life.*

*Andrew Jackson was elected president in 1828. He and Buchanan shared many ideas about how the U.S. government should work.*

For many years, the Missouri Compromise seemed to work. Unfortunately, it would not be enough to keep both sides happy forever. The Compromise made it clear that there were strong differences between slaveholders and Americans who were against slavery.

In 1828, Andrew Jackson was elected president. Jackson and Buchanan were members of the same **political party,** the Democratic Party. That same year, Buchanan was reelected to the House of Representatives. He supported Jackson in any way he could, helping him accomplish the goals of their party. In 1831, President Jackson offered Buchanan the post of **minister** to Russia. In this position, Buchanan would be in charge of U.S. relations with Russia.

Buchanan was unsure whether he wanted to accept the president's offer. For one thing, he didn't speak French. At the time, French was the language spoken by diplomats. Diplomats are government officials like Buchanan who represent their country in

discussions with other nations. But Buchanan finally accepted the job, and he began taking French lessons. In March of 1832, he left for St. Petersburg, the capital of Russia.

Buchanan arrived in Russia in late spring. He found life there to be very different from that in the United States. The chilly June weather forced him to wear a warm cloak, even in the daytime. Yet at that time of year, the sky was so bright and the days so long that he could read without a candle until midnight.

*Washington, D.C., looked very different when Buchanan was in the House of Representatives. There were few buildings, and much of the area was still farmland. The White House is at left in this photograph. The Capitol is in the background at right.*

*Buchanan was unhappy in the city of St. Petersburg. He missed the United States and its freedoms. He also wanted to be closer to his family.*

Still, he thought it was strange to live in a country with so many restrictions about what one could say or do. He wrote to President Jackson that "there is no freedom of the press, no public opinion, and but little political conversation." The Russian people worried that they would be punished if they spoke out against their government. As an American who was guaranteed freedom of speech by the **Constitution,** this was difficult for Buchanan to understand.

16

While in St. Petersburg, Buchanan made an agreement that allowed the United States to use Russia's Black Sea as a trade route. It took several months before Russian leaders agreed to sign the treaty, but Buchanan finally convinced them. About the same time, Great Britain also wanted to make such an agreement with Russia. But their minister could not reach an agreement with the Russian government.

In 1833, Buchanan asked President Jackson for permission to return home. He found the cold Russian winters difficult, and he longed to see his family again. Although Buchanan's mother had died in the spring of that year, he did not receive the news until July. This made him feel that he was too far from home. He also had heard that Pennsylvania's citizens wanted him to run for the Senate. In August, he began the long journey home.

The next year, Buchanan was elected to the U.S. Senate. The two main issues during his time as a senator were banking and slavery. Buchanan argued fiercely against a new law that Senator Henry Clay had suggested. It would allow people who owed large amounts of money to declare bankruptcy. This meant that people

## Interesting Facts

▸ As a **politician,**
Buchanan had to
spend much of the
year in Washington.
The city resembled
a small farm town
rather than a nation's
capital. Chickens,
geese, and pigs
wandered the streets.
Canals and water-
ways gave off a foul
odor. No wonder
Buchanan escaped to
his Pennsylvania estate
whenever he could!

could be freed from their **debts** by going to court and asking for the government's help. Buchanan was against the idea. He thought it would create too much work for the nation's courts and cost the government too much money. He believed that bankruptcy would make it too easy for people to borrow money without ever paying it back. Even though he felt sorry for people with money problems, he was more concerned with upholding the law.

The problem of slavery became ever more troublesome during the 20 years before the **Civil War.** Although Buchanan did not like slavery, he believed that slaveholders had certain rights. Southern states had been admitted to the Union years before as slave states. How could the government take away that right so many years later? In addition, slaves were considered property, just like a house or livestock. The U.S. Constitution protects people's belongings. Buchanan thought that taking away property from the nation's citizens was a dangerous thing for a government to do—even if that "property" was a human being. He believed that the states should have the right to decide whether to allow slavery.

Buchanan respected the laws of the Constitution, so he supported the slave owners. He saw no way to forbid slavery in the Southern states without damaging the Union. Even though he did not like the fact that one human being could own another, he did not join forces with the **abolitionists** who were against slavery. His main concern was keeping the Union together.

In the election of 1844, Democrats in Pennsylvania wanted Buchanan to run for president instead of a Southerner named James K. Polk. But Buchanan knew he did not have enough support from people in other states. He planned to remain in the Senate. But when Polk became president, he chose Buchanan as the secretary of state. This put him in charge of the nation's **foreign affairs.** Although Buchanan had been re-elected to the Senate, he gave up his seat and accepted President Polk's offer.

*President Polk (below) believed that Buchanan's experience in St. Petersburg would make him an excellent secretary of state. In this position, Buchanan was responsible for U.S. relations with other countries.*

WHEN JAMES POLK WAS president, Buchanan served as secretary of state, even though he had hoped to be named to the Supreme Court, the most powerful court in the nation. But President Polk wanted Buchanan to manage the nation's foreign affairs.

One problem at the time was whether Texas, an independent **republic,** would become part of the United States. Mexico also wanted control of the area. In 1845, Britain and France advised the Texas government not to join the Union. They tried to convince Texas leaders to sign a treaty with Mexico. In this treaty, Mexico would agree to let Texas remain independent if it promised not to join the United States. Britain and France did not want the United States to become more powerful in North America than it already was. If Texas were an independent nation, it might have helped keep Americans from expanding even farther across the continent.

20

The people of Texas were against the treaty. In fact, most of them wanted to join the Union. Texas joined the Union in December of 1845.

Then a new dispute arose as to where the border between Mexico and Texas lay. Texans asked the United States for help when Mexicans gathered along Texas's southern border. On April 25, 1846, Mexico fired the first shot of the Mexican War. For the next two years, Generals Zachary Taylor and Winfield Scott fought their way across Mexico. When they captured Mexico City, the capital, the enemy was forced to give up. President Polk wanted to take over the whole country, but Buchanan convinced him to accept another option. In the end, a treaty gave the United States a huge piece of land. It increased the nation's size by nearly 1.2 million square miles. Today the territory acquired after the war makes up the states of Arizona, Nevada, California, and Utah, as well as parts of New Mexico, Colorado, and Wyoming.

# Chapter THREE

# Approaching Storm

*Buchanan wanted to run for president in 1848 and again in 1852, but the Democratic Party chose other candidates. He finally had his chance in 1856.*

IN 1848, BUCHANAN CONSIDERED RUNNING for president, but the Democratic Party chose Lewis Cass instead. General Zachary Taylor, who had helped win the Mexican War that same year, won the election. By this time, Buchanan was tired of Washington politics. He purchased Wheatland, a 22-acre estate, and returned to the Pennsylvania countryside. Although he never married, he enjoyed spending time with his nieces and nephews and their children.

Buchanan did not lose touch with his political friends in Washington. Many still came to visit him at Wheatland, seeking his advice on government matters. By 1852, he was ready to return to politics—and to run for president.

The problem of slavery continued. When the United States took over land in the West after the Mexican War, the country had to decide whether to allow slavery there. Congress had created the Compromise of 1850 to try to solve the problem. It allowed California to enter the Union as a free state. The other western territories of New Mexico and Utah could decide whether to allow

*Congressmen from the North and the South bitterly debated whether to allow slavery in the new territories that the United States took over after the Mexican War. Senator Henry Clay (standing at center) suggested a compromise to Congress in 1850. He hoped it would hold the Union together.*

*As part of the Compromise of 1850, Northern congressmen agreed to enforce the Fugitive Slave Law. This required that the North return all runaway slaves, like those shown in the drawing below, to their Southern owners. Northerners could not help slaves escape to freedom. But they refused to obey the law and continued to help runaway slaves until slavery was finally abolished after the Civil War.*

slavery for themselves. Buchanan believed this was wrong. He thought Congress should enforce the Missouri Compromise of 1820. This allowed slavery in areas south of a specific latitude (36 degrees, 30 minutes), including the new territories of the West.

Buchanan didn't win the presidential **nomination** from the Democrats. They chose Franklin Pierce, another general from the Mexican War. Pierce became the next president.

Pierce offered Buchanan the post of minister to Great Britain. Buchanan's niece, Harriet Lane, joined him there in 1854. Harriet had gone to live with her uncle after the death of her parents many years before. They had grown close over the years, and she was now a charming young lady. The British people admired her. Even Queen Victoria was delighted by Harriet's friendly personality.

Buchanan's service as minister to Great Britain was disappointing. He had hoped to encourage the British to stop setting up colonies in the Americas. But Great Britain was involved in a war with Russia, and its leaders were too busy to consider the issue.

By 1856, Buchanan was ready to return home. While he was away, the strain between the North and the South had increased. He left Britain in February and arrived to find his country in turmoil. The problem was most severe in Kansas. In 1854, the Kansas-Nebraska Act had been passed. It allowed the settlers of these territories to accept or outlaw slavery, depending on what they wanted.

The right of citizens to choose slavery or freedom was first tested in Kansas.

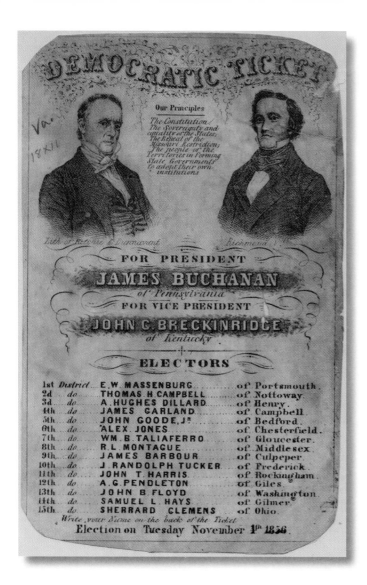

*The Democrats chose Buchanan as their presidential candidate for the election of 1856.*

Abolitionists from the North organized groups of settlers to move to the territory. When word reached pro-slavery people, they sent their own groups to Kansas. There seemed no way to avoid a conflict. Pro-slavery and abolitionist forces battled in Kansas, leaving more than 200 people dead.

Buchanan believed he could find a way to end the serious problems his nation faced. He felt the time was right to seek the presidential nomination for the 1856 election. Much of the country seemed to agree. Buchanan was personally against slavery and a Northerner, so some people in the North voted for him. But he supported the right to own slaves, so many Southerners voted for him as well. Buchanan ran against John C. Fremont and won by 500,000 votes—more than 58 percent of the vote.

DRED SCOTT WAS A SLAVE OWNED BY DR. JOHN Emerson of Missouri. Emerson was a surgeon with the U.S. Army. In 1834, the army sent Emerson to Illinois, where slavery was against the law. He did not think he had to obey anti-slavery laws if the army sent him to a free state, so he took Scott with him. Later, they moved to what is now Minnesota. Slavery was also illegal there. Finally, in 1838, Emerson and Scott returned to Missouri.

Scott decided that because he had lived in a free state and territory for four years, he should be considered a free man. In 1846, he went to court in Missouri to sue for his freedom. He won the case, but the Emerson family appealed the decision. This meant they asked a more powerful court to consider the case. Eventually, in 1857, the case reached the U.S. Supreme Court.

The nine justices (judges) of the Supreme Court were mostly from the South. They decided that Scott was still a slave. They said traveling through free areas did not make a slave free. For one thing, the Constitution made it illegal to take property away from any citizen. Since slaves were property, they could not be taken from their owners, regardless of whether they crossed into free territory. The justices also stated that the Constitution never included blacks as citizens of the United States. Only a citizen can take a case to court in the United States. So Scott did not even have the right to sue for his freedom. Worst of all, the chief justice said that blacks were inferior to whites. For that reason, African Americans "had no rights which the white man was bound to respect."

Scott was terribly disappointed by the decision. But soon after, he was sold to Peter Blow, the son of his first owner. Blow freed him immediately. After a long battle for liberty, Scott was finally a free man.

# Chapter FOUR

# A Wearisome Presidency

*Buchanan's niece, Harriet, acted as the first lady while he was in office.*

ON MARCH 4, 1857, JAMES BUCHANAN AND Vice President John Breckinridge arrived to take the oath of office at the Capitol. Most Americans believed that Buchanan was a good politician. They hoped he could solve the problems between the North and the South. At his **inauguration,** he said that there was a simple solution to the slavery issue.

As always, Buchanan was on the side of the law. He said that the U.S. Constitution protected slavery in the South, where it had always existed. If these states allowed slavery, how could the **federal** government outlaw it anywhere else in the country? Buchanan said that new territories should decide the issue for themselves. It was the only way to solve the problem without disobeying the Constitution.

Buchanan's argument was logical and correct by law. But it did not recognize the fact that a growing number of Americans hated slavery. They believed slavery was always wrong. They wanted it to be outlawed everywhere, even in the South where it had existed for hundreds of years. Buchanan's stand on slavery would cause problems for

*President Buchanan said that the issue of slavery could be solved once and for all if Americans gave the slave states the only thing they wanted—to be left alone. But many Americans could not bear to live in a nation that allowed slavery.*

him throughout his presidency. It would also lead the nation closer than ever to civil war.

Almost immediately, Buchanan had to face the slavery problem in Kansas. He began by selecting a cabinet, the group of men who would advise him. He tried to choose people from both the North and the South. He also wanted advisers who would strive to save the Union. Unfortunately, most of his cabinet did not want to end slavery.

Meanwhile, the problems in Kansas continued. Two years earlier, voters had chosen representatives for their legislature. Supporters of slavery won the election. Something was wrong, however. Only residents of Kansas could vote in the election. Abolitionists learned that pro-slavery voters had traveled to Kansas from Missouri to cast illegal votes. They said the election should not count. They asked that Kansas be admitted as a free state.

When Buchanan entered office in 1857, the problem had not been solved. He supported the pro-slavery legislature. He said the government had been set up by its citizens, just as those of other territories had been.

Buchanan named pro-slavery leader Robert Walker the governor of the Kansas territory. In October of 1857, a meeting was held to create the territory's constitution. Abolitionists refused to attend. They said there were too many pro-slavery leaders at the meeting. So the delegates created the Kansas constitution, and one part of it allowed slavery. It still had to be accepted by all citizens, but the abolitionists refused to vote on it. President Buchanan decided that the constitution was legal. He urged Congress to admit Kansas to the Union as a slave state. Congress refused to do so until all the people of Kansas decided whether to accept the constitution. In 1858, the citizens of Kansas voted on it again. It was rejected by a large number of votes.

The division between the North and the South grew still more serious in the last two years of Buchanan's presidency. In 1859, an abolitionist named John Brown and his followers attacked a Virginia arsenal, where the government stored weapons. He planned to use the weapons to start a slave **rebellion.** Federal troops stopped the uprising and captured Brown. He was found guilty of treason and put to death. The event stirred up feelings about slavery all over the nation. Some Northerners felt that Brown was a good man for having fought so hard for what was right. Southerners believed he was a criminal. It was one more step on the road to war.

President Buchanan did have some success, mostly in the area of foreign affairs. He helped create a treaty that forced the British to stop setting up colonies in the Americas. It also made them agree to stop attacking U.S. ships in the Gulf of Mexico. When American ships were attacked off the coast of Paraguay, Buchanan sent in the U.S. Navy to fight back. Paraguay's government signed a treaty stating that it would no longer attack American ships.

Even with these accomplishments, Buchanan had other problems in addition to slavery. Congressman John Covode of Pennsylvania accused Buchanan of using his money to make other leaders pass certain laws. He said that Congress should **impeach** the president. Although the House spent several months looking into the matter, no evidence of wrongdoing was found.

The election of 1860 was fast approaching. By this time, Buchanan simply wanted to leave the nation's problems to someone else. He realized he had little chance of receiving the Democratic Party's nomination. The Northern Democrats nominated Congressman Stephen A. Douglas. Southern Democrats nominated Vice President Breckinridge, whom Buchanan supported. But this split within the Democratic Party caused problems. It helped Abraham Lincoln, their opponent from the Republican Party, win the election.

Southerners were sure that Lincoln would try to end slavery. In December of 1860, before he even became president, South Carolina **seceded** from the Union. In the final months of his presidency, Buchanan refused

▶ One important
thing that Buchanan
achieved was to
prevent four slave
states from leaving
the Union: Delaware,
Kentucky, Maryland,
and Missouri. These
states became known
as the "border states"
because they repre-
sented the boundary
between the Union
and the Southern
Confederacy. These
states continued
to allow slavery
throughout the war.

South Carolina's request to remove Union soldiers from a Union fort in Charleston called Fort Sumter. But Congress refused to send more soldiers to defend it. Soon, several of Buchanan's cabinet members left their positions. Last efforts in Congress to reach a compromise failed. The nation prepared for war and waited to see what would happen next.

By February, six more states had seceded. Buchanan could only bide his time until Lincoln took office. On March 4, 1861, the two men rode toward the Capitol for Lincoln's inauguration. Buchanan turned to the president-elect and said, "If you are as happy, my dear sir, on entering the White House as I am in leaving it and returning home, you are the happiest man in this country!"

The Civil War began on April 12, when Southern troops fired on Fort Sumter. Buchanan supported most of Lincoln's decisions during the war. But he was still the target of several threats. Some people believed the war was Buchanan's fault. He finally wrote a book in his defense titled *Mr. Buchanan's Administration on the Eve of the Rebellion*. It was published in 1866. Unfortunately, few people read it.

James Buchanan's final years were spent at Wheatland. He entertained friends and family, read, and worked for his favorite charity. He died quietly on June 1, 1868. On the day before his death, he told a friend, "I have no regret for any public act of my life, and history will **vindicate** my memory."

Today Buchanan is remembered as a poor leader who could not solve the serious problems his nation faced. But he entered the presidency at one of the most trying times in American history. Unfortunately, he was not up to the challenge.

*This political cartoon expresses the artist's opinion about James Buchanan's presidency. It depicts a stately eagle, the national bird, as it appeared when Buchanan entered office. Next to it is the same bird, starving and ill, when Buchanan left office in 1861.*

ALTHOUGH BUCHANAN never married, few presidents have had a more charming and outgoing "first lady." Buchanan's niece, Harriet Lane, took charge of the duties that usually belong to a president's wife.

At the age of 11, both of Harriet's parents died. She chose Buchanan to be her guardian. From then on, she called him "Nunc," a nickname for uncle. He called her his "mischievous romp of a niece." She easily won over British royalty and citizens when she served as Buchanan's companion during his service as minister to Great Britain. When he became president, Buchanan asked Harriet to accompany him to the White House. There she acted as hostess and oversaw the housekeeping.

When Buchanan held important dinner parties for government leaders, Harriet planned the seating arrangements so that no political enemies sat next to each other. She entertained the first Japanese delegation to the United States. She hosted a dinner party, games, and a trip down the Potomac River for the Prince of Wales, who later became King Edward VIII of England.

Harriet served her country in many ways. She helped establish a national art gallery and worked tirelessly to help improve living conditions for Native Americans. Some people called her the "Great Mother of the Indians."

After leaving the White House, Harriet continued to care for Buchanan until 1866. Then she married a Baltimore banker, Henry Elliott Johnston. They had two sons, but both died in their teens. Her husband passed away shortly after.

Harriet returned to Washington, where she worked to obtain hospital care for needy children and also gave money to help establish what is now the National Museum of American Art. Harriet Lane Johnston died on July 3, 1903, at the age of 73.

*1791* James Buchanan is born in Cove Gap, Pennsylvania, on April 23.

*1796* The Buchanan family moves to Mercersburg, where Buchanan's father builds a home and general store.

*1807* At age 16, Buchanan enters Dickinson College.

*1809* After graduating from college, Buchanan decides to become a lawyer. His father sends him to the town of Lancaster to work for a lawyer while he studies law.

*1812* Buchanan opens a law office in Lancaster.

*1814* For a few weeks, Buchanan fights as a volunteer in the War of 1812. In November, he is elected to the Pennsylvania House of Representatives.

*1815* Buchanan is reelected to the legislature.

*1816* Buchanan leaves politics and returns to his law practice.

*1819* Buchanan asks Ann Coleman to marry him. After hearing false rumors that he is marrying Ann for her money, the Coleman family ends the engagement. Ann dies later that year. Buchanan is heartbroken.

*1820* Buchanan runs for the U.S. House of Representatives. He wins the election and goes on to serve five terms. The Missouri Compromise is created to solve problems between the North and the South. It allows Missouri to enter the Union as a slave state, while Maine enters as a free state. This means that there are an equal number of slave and free states in the Union. The Compromise also states that slavery is legal south of a specific latitude.

*1831* President Andrew Jackson names Buchanan minister to Russia.

*1832* Buchanan leaves for St. Petersburg, the Russian capital. He succeeds in negotiating a treaty with Russia that allows U.S. ships to travel the Black Sea.

*1833* Buchanan travels back to the United States.

*1834* Pennsylvania voters elect Buchanan to the U.S. Senate.

*1845* Buchanan leaves the Senate to serve as President Polk's secretary of state.

*1846* The Mexican War begins.

**1848** Buchanan leaves politics and purchases Wheatland, his 22-acre estate. The United States defeats Mexico and gains more than a million square miles of land.

**1850** The Compromise of 1850 allows California to enter the Union as a free state, while New Mexico and Utah may decide for themselves whether to allow slavery.

**1853** President Pierce names Buchanan minister to Great Britain.

**1854** While Buchanan is in Great Britain, the Kansas-Nebraska Act is passed, separating the Nebraska Territory into what will later become two states. Settlers in each place will decide whether to allow slavery.

**1855** Problems develop in the Kansas Territory between abolitionists and people who support slavery.

**1856** Buchanan returns from Great Britain. He decides to run for the presidency. Abolitionist and pro-slavery forces continue to battle in Kansas.

**1857** Buchanan is inaugurated as the 15th president of the United States on March 4. In his inaugural address, he says that the federal government should not decide whether to outlaw slavery in individual states. Two days after he enters office, the Supreme Court rules that Dred Scott, a slave, cannot sue for his freedom. It also declares that black slaves are not considered U.S. citizens and that the federal government cannot outlaw slavery in individual states.

**1859** John Brown raids the arsenal at Harper's Ferry, Virginia. Representative John Covode asks Congress to impeach President Buchanan.

**1860** Abraham Lincoln is elected president in November. South Carolina secedes from the Union the following month.

**1861** By February, six more Southern states have seceded from the Union. In April, Southern forces fire on Fort Sumter, the Union's fort. The Civil War begins.

**1865** The Civil War ends.

**1866** Buchanan publishes a defense of his presidency, *Mr. Buchanan's Administration on the Eve of the Rebellion.*

**1868** James Buchanan dies at Wheatland on June 1.

**abolitionists (ab-uh-LISH-uh-nists)**
Abolitionists were people who wanted to end slavery. Buchanan did not like slavery, but he was not an abolitionist.

**civil war (SIV-il WAR)**
A civil war is a war between opposing groups of citizens within the same country. The Civil War began after the South seceded from the Union.

**compromise (KOM-pruh-myz)**
A compromise is a way to settle a disagreement in which both sides give up part of what they want. Congress agreed to the Missouri Compromise in 1820.

**constitution (kon-stih-TOO-shun)**
A constitution is the set of basic principles that govern a state, country, or society. The U.S. Constitution guarantees freedom of speech for Americans.

**debts (DETZ)**
Debts are amounts of money that people owe. Buchanan did not believe that people should ask the government to pay their debts.

**federal (FED-er-ul)**
Federal means having to do with the central government of the United States, rather than a state or city government. Many people believed the federal government did not have the right to outlaw slavery.

**foreign affairs (FOR-en uh-FAIRZ)**
Foreign affairs are matters involving other countries. As secretary of state, Buchanan was in charge of foreign affairs.

**impeach (im-PEECH)**
If the House of Representatives votes to impeach a president, it charges him (or her) with a crime or serious misdeed. Representative John Covode wanted to impeach Buchanan.

**inauguration (ih-nawg-yuh-RAY-shun)**
An inauguration is the ceremony that takes place when a new president begins a term. Buchanan gave a speech at his inauguration in 1857.

**latitude (LAT-ih-tood)**
Lines of latitude are imaginary lines that circle the Earth and are used on maps and globes for measurement. Lines of latitude are equal distances apart from each other and measure distance from the equator.

**minister (MIN-ih-stir)**
A minister is a person who is in charge of one part of the government. The minister to Russia is in charge of U.S. relations with Russia.

**nomination (nom-ih-NAY-shun)**
If someone receives a nomination, he or she is chosen by a political party to run for an office. Buchanan won the presidential nomination from the Democratic Party in 1856.

**political party
(puh-LIT-ih-kul PAR-tee)**
A political party is a group of people who share similar ideas about how to run a government. Buchanan was a member of the Democratic Party.

**politician (pawl-ih-TISH-un)**
A politician is a person who holds an office in government. Most Americans believed Buchanan was a good politician.

**rebellion (reh-BEL-yen)**
A rebellion is a fight against one's government. Abolitionist John Brown wanted to start a slave rebellion.

**republic (ree-PUB-lik)**
A republic is a nation with a government elected by its citizens. Texas was an independent republic after the Texas Revolution.

**secede (suh-SEED)**
If a group secedes, it separates from a larger group. South Carolina was the first Southern state to secede from the Union.

**term (TERM)**
A term of office is the length of time politicians can keep their positions by law. A president's term is four years.

**territory (TAIR-ih-tor-ee)**
A territory is a piece of land or a region, especially land that belongs to a government. The Missouri Compromise was supposed to apply to new territories in the West.

**union (YOON-yen)**
A union is the joining together of two people or groups of people, such as states. The Union is another name for the United States.

**vindicate (VIN-dih-kayt)**
To vindicate someone means to clear him or her from dishonor or the charge of wrongdoing. Buchanan said that history would vindicate his memory.

# *Our* PRESIDENTS

| President | Birthplace | Life Span | Presidency | Political Party | First Lady |
|-----------|------------|-----------|------------|-----------------|------------|
| George Washington | Virginia | 1732–1799 | 1789–1797 | None | Martha Dandridge Custis Washington |
| John Adams | Massachusetts | 1735–1826 | 1797–1801 | Federalist | Abigail Smith Adams |
| Thomas Jefferson | Virginia | 1743–1826 | 1801–1809 | Democratic-Republican | widower |
| James Madison | Virginia | 1751–1836 | 1809–1817 | Democratic Republican | Dolley Payne Todd Madison |
| James Monroe | Virginia | 1758–1831 | 1817–1825 | Democratic Republican | Elizabeth Kortright Monroe |
| John Quincy Adams | Massachusetts | 1767–1848 | 1825–1829 | Democratic-Republican | Louisa Johnson Adams |
| Andrew Jackson | South Carolina | 1767–1845 | 1829–1837 | Democrat | widower |
| Martin Van Buren | New York | 1782–1862 | 1837–1841 | Democrat | widower |
| William H. Harrison | Virginia | 1773–1841 | 1841 | Whig | Anna Symmes Harrison |
| John Tyler | Virginia | 1790–1862 | 1841–1845 | Whig | Letitia Christian Tyler / Julia Gardiner Tyler |
| James K. Polk | North Carolina | 1795–1849 | 1845–1849 | Democrat | Sarah Childress Polk |

# *Our* PRESIDENTS

| President | Birthplace | Life Span | Presidency | Political Party | First Lady |
|---|---|---|---|---|---|
| Zachary Taylor | Virginia | 1784–1850 | 1849–1850 | Whig | Margaret Mackall Smith Taylor |
| Millard Fillmore | New York | 1800–1874 | 1850–1853 | Whig | Abigail Powers Fillmore |
| Franklin Pierce | New Hampshire | 1804–1869 | 1853–1857 | Democrat | Jane Means Appleton Pierce |
| James Buchanan | Pennsylvania | 1791–1868 | 1857–1861 | Democrat | never married |
| Abraham Lincoln | Kentucky | 1809–1865 | 1861–1865 | Republican | Mary Todd Lincoln |
| Andrew Johnson | North Carolina | 1808–1875 | 1865–1869 | Democrat | Eliza McCardle Johnson |
| Ulysses S. Grant | Ohio | 1822–1885 | 1869–1877 | Republican | Julia Dent Grant |
| Rutherford B. Hayes | Ohio | 1822–1893 | 1877–1881 | Republican | Lucy Webb Hayes |
| James A. Garfield | Ohio | 1831–1881 | 1881 | Republican | Lucretia Rudolph Garfield |
| Chester A. Arthur | Vermont | 1829–1886 | 1881–1885 | Republican | widower |
| Grover Cleveland | New Jersey | 1837–1908 | 1885–1889 | Democrat | Frances Folsom Cleveland |

# *Our* PRESIDENTS

| President | Birthplace | Life Span | Presidency | Political Party | First Lady |
|---|---|---|---|---|---|
| Benjamin Harrison | Ohio | 1833–1901 | 1889–1893 | Republican | Caroline Scott Harrison |
| Grover Cleveland | New Jersey | 1837–1908 | 1893–1897 | Democrat | Frances Folsom Cleveland |
| William McKinley | Ohio | 1843–1901 | 1897–1901 | Republican | Ida Saxton McKinley |
| Theodore Roosevelt | New York | 1858–1919 | 1901–1909 | Republican | Edith Kermit Carow Roosevelt |
| William H. Taft | Ohio | 1857–1930 | 1909–1913 | Republican | Helen Herron Taft |
| Woodrow Wilson | Virginia | 1856–1924 | 1913–1921 | Democrat | Ellen L. Axson Wilson<br>Edith Bolling Galt Wilson |
| Warren G. Harding | Ohio | 1865–1923 | 1921–1923 | Republican | Florence Kling De Wolfe Harding |
| Calvin Coolidge | Vermont | 1872–1933 | 1923–1929 | Republican | Grace Goodhue Coolidge |
| Herbert C. Hoover | Iowa | 1874–1964 | 1929–1933 | Republican | Lou Henry Hoover |
| Franklin D. Roosevelt | New York | 1882–1945 | 1933–1945 | Democrat | Anna Eleanor Roosevelt Roosevelt |
| Harry S. Truman | Missouri | 1884–1972 | 1945–1953 | Democrat | Elizabeth Wallace Truman |

# *Our* PRESIDENTS

| President | Birthplace | Life Span | Presidency | Political Party | First Lady |
|-----------|-----------|-----------|------------|-----------------|------------|
| Dwight D. Eisenhower | Texas | 1890–1969 | 1953–1961 | Republican | Mary "Mamie" Doud Eisenhower |
| John F. Kennedy | Massachusetts | 1917–1963 | 1961–1963 | Democrat | Jacqueline Bouvier Kennedy |
| Lyndon B. Johnson | Texas | 1908–1973 | 1963–1969 | Democrat | Claudia Alta Taylor Johnson |
| Richard M. Nixon | California | 1913–1994 | 1969–1974 | Republican | Thelma Catherine Ryan Nixon |
| Gerald Ford | Nebraska | 1913– | 1974–1977 | Republican | Elizabeth "Betty" Bloomer Warren Ford |
| James Carter | Georgia | 1924– | 1977–1981 | Democrat | Rosalynn Smith Carter |
| Ronald Reagan | Illinois | 1911– | 1981–1989 | Republican | Nancy Davis Reagan |
| George Bush | Massachusetts | 1924– | 1989–1993 | Republican | Barbara Pierce Bush |
| William Clinton | Arkansas | 1946– | 1993–2001 | Democrat | Hillary Rodham Clinton |
| George W. Bush | Connecticut | 1946– | 2001– | Republican | Laura Welch Bush |

# *Presidential* FACTS

### Qualifications

To run for president, a candidate must
- be at least 35 years old
- be a citizen who was born in the United States
- have lived in the United States for 14 years

### Term of Office

A president's term of office is four years. No president can stay in office for more than two terms.

### Election Date

The presidential election takes place every four years on the first Tuesday of November.

### Inauguration Date

Presidents are inaugurated on January 20.

### Oath of Office

I do solemnly swear I will faithfully execute the office of the President of the United States and will to the best of my ability preserve, protect, and defend the Constitution of the United States.

### Write a Letter to the President

One of the best things about being a U.S. citizen is that Americans get to participate in their government. They can speak out if they feel government leaders aren't doing their jobs. They can also praise leaders who are going the extra mile. Do you have something you'd like the president to do? Should the president worry more about the environment and encourage people to recycle? Should the government spend more money on our schools? You can write a letter to the president to say how you feel!

1600 Pennsylvania Avenue
Washington, D.C. 20500

You can even send an e-mail to: president@whitehouse.gov

# For Further INFORMATION

*Internet Sites*

Find more information and links to Web sites about President Buchanan:
http://www.pcntv.com/buchanan.htm

Visit Wheatland, Buchanan's home:
http://www.wheatland.org/home.html

Find historical resources about the Civil War, including time lines and life stories:
http://www.americancivilwar.com

Find a children's listing of Civil War sites:
www.kidinfo.com/American_History/Civil_War.html

Learn more about the Compromise of 1850 and other acts leading to the Civil War:
http://www.loc.gov/exhibits/treasures/trm043.html
http://www.wwnorton.com/college/history/ushist/timeline/comp1850.htm
http://www.worldbook.com/fun/aajourny/html/bh115.html

Learn more about all the presidents and visit the White House:
http://www.whitehouse.gov/WH/glimpse/presidents/html/presidents.html
http://www.thepresidency.org/presinfo.htm
http://www.americanpresidents.org/

*Books*

Brill, Marlene Targ. *James Buchanan (Encyclopedia of Presidents)*. Chicago: Childrens Press, 1988.

Graham, Martin F., Richard A. Sauers, and George Skoch. *The Blue and the Gray*. Lincolnwood, IL: Publications International, 1996.

Lester, Julius. *To Be a Slave*. New York: Scholastic, 1968.

Shelly, Mary V., and Sandra H. Munroe Shelly. *Harriet Lane, First Lady of the White House*. Sutter House, 1980.

# Index

abolitionists, 19, 24, 26, 30-31, 39

bankruptcy, 17-18
Black Sea, 17, 38
Blow, Peter, 27
border states, 34
Breckinridge, John, 28, 33
Brooks, Preston, 25
Brown, John, 32, 39
Buchanan, Elizabeth Speer, 6
Buchanan, James
   blame for Civil War, 34
   death of, 35, 39
   education of, 6-8
   foreign affairs policies, 32-33
   law career, 8-11, 38
   as minister to Great Britain, 25
   as minister to Russia, 14-17, 38
   as Pennsylvania state representative, 9-10, 38
   as president, 28-33
   as secretary of state, 19-21, 38
   as soldier in War of 1812, 9, 38
   solution to slavery issues, 28-29
   as U.S. representative, 12, 14, 38
   as U.S. senator, 17-19, 38
Buchanan, James (father), 6, 38
Butler, Andrew, 25

California, 21, 23, 39
Cass, Lewis, 22
Civil War, 18, 33-34, 39
Clay, Henry, 17, 23
Coleman, Ann, 10-11, 38
Compromise of 1850, 23-24, 39
Covode, John, 33, 39
Crandall, Prudence, 14

Democratic Party, 14, 19, 22, 26, 33
Douglas, Stephen A., 33

Emerson, John, 27

Fort Sumter, 34, 39
France, 20
Fremont, John C., 26
Fugitive Slave Law, 24

Great Britain, 9, 17, 20, 25, 32, 36, 39
Jackson, Andrew, 10, 14, 16, 38
Johnson, Andrew, 33
Johnston, Henry Elliott, 37

Kansas, 25-26, 30-31
Kansas-Nebraska Act, 25, 39
King, John, 7-8
King, Rufus, 31

Lane, Harriet, 25, 28, 36-37
Lincoln, Abraham, 33-34, 39

Maine, 12-13, 38
Mexican War, 20-24, 38
Missouri Compromise of 1820, 12-14, 24, 38

New Mexico, 21, 23-24, 39

Pierce, Franklin, 24-25, 39
Polk, James K., 19-21, 38

Republican Party, 33
Russia, 14-17, 25, 38

Scott, Dred, 27, 39
Scott, Winfield, 21
slavery issues, 12-14, 17-19, 23-32, 38, 39
South Carolina, 33-34, 39
Sumner, Charles, 25
Supreme Court, 20, 27, 39

Taylor, Zachary, 21-22
Texas, 20-21

Union
   border states, 34
   boundary between North and South, 13
   foreign affairs, 19-21, 32-33
   free and slave states, 12-13, 18, 23-25, 38
   secession from, 33-34, 39
U.S. Constitution, 16, 18-19, 27-29
Utah, 21, 23-24

Walker, Robert, 31
War of 1812, 9, 38
Washington, D.C., 9, 15, 18
Wheatland, 22, 35, 39